An A-

ACTIVITY BO

INDOOR FUN

By Meg Sanders & Kate Crocker

Illustrated by
Charlotte Stowell

Kingfisher Books

A is for acrobat

To make this colourful acrobat,
you will need:

- Some tracing paper
- Card
- Crayons or paints
- Scissors
- Four split pins
- A lollipop stick
- Sticky tape

1. Trace arms, legs and body onto card. Colour them in, cut out carefully, and make the holes – a hole puncher is best for this.

2. Fix the arms and legs to the body with the pins, so that they move quite easily. Now tape the stick to the back of the acrobat.

1

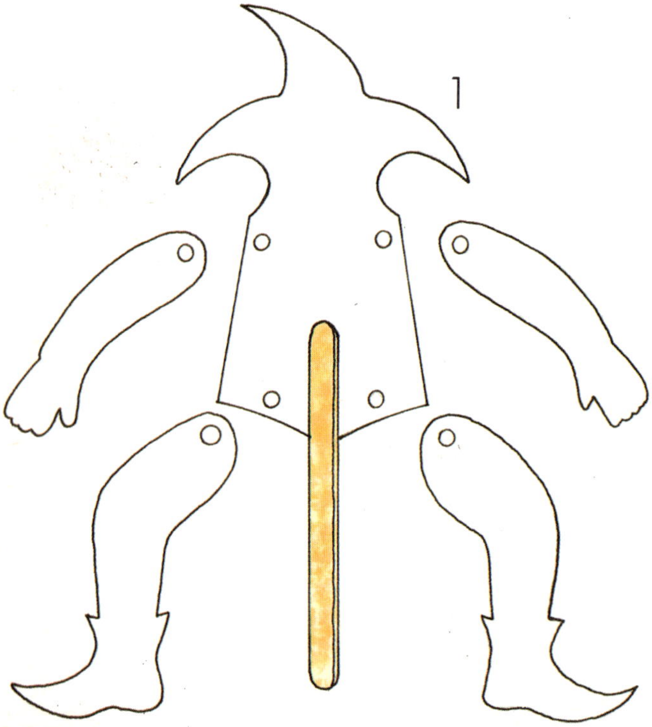

2

NOTE TO PARENTS: THE ACTIVITIES IN THIS BOOK HAVE BEEN DESIGNED FOR ADULTS AND CHILDREN TO DO TOGETHER

Shake the stick up and down, and from side to side – and watch the acrobat perform his dance!

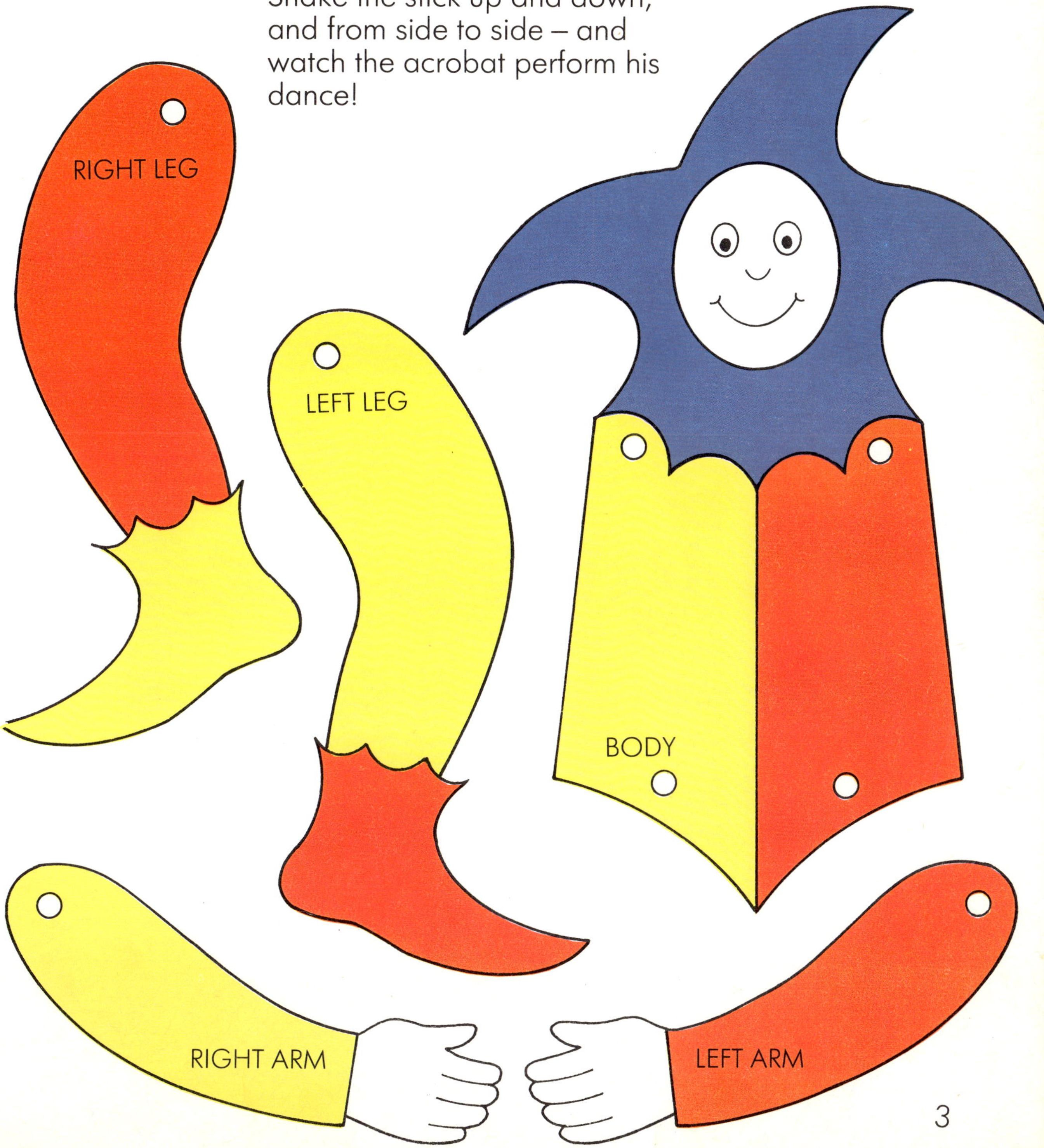

B is for bubbles

To make really giant bubbles, you will need:

A bottle of bubble-blowing liquid
2 tablespoons glycerine
2 tablespoons washing-up liquid
About 30 centimetres thin wire

Ask an adult to bend the wire into a giant loop, like the one shown here. Mix up all your ingredients in a shallow bowl, and gently dip your giant loop in and out of the liquid. Don't blow – just wave the loop around in the air to make megabubbles!

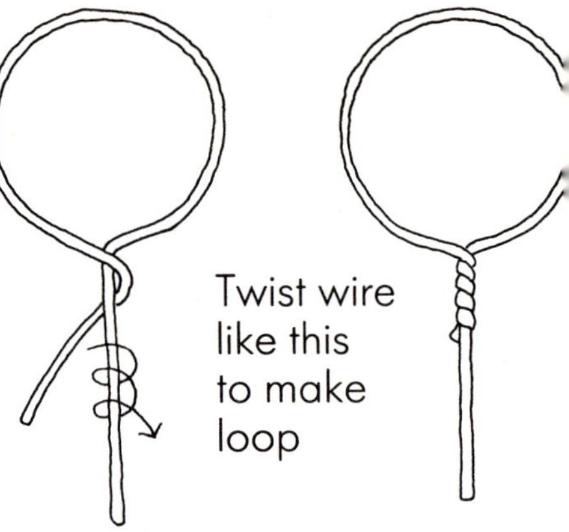

C is for chocolate

Cooking with chocolate is always special! You will need an adult's help with these two recipes.

CHOCOLATE ICE-CREAM CUPS
120 grams chocolate Ice-cream
5 dried apricots 10 almonds

Melt the chocolate in an ovenproof bowl over a pan of hot water. Chop up the apricots and almonds, and add to the chocolate.

Use the mixture to line paper cake cases, and leave to set in the fridge. Later, top up with ice-cream, and serve at once!

CHOCOLATE FUDGE
120 grams plain chocolate
60 grams butter
2 tablespoons milk
500 grams icing sugar
1 teaspoon vanilla essence

Melt chocolate and butter in an ovenproof bowl over a pan of hot water. Take off the heat and stir in milk, sugar and vanilla. Spoon mixture into a shallow tin, and leave somewhere cool to set.

D is for disguise

Amaze your family and friends with these foolproof disguises!

FALSE GLASSES AND NOSE
You will need five pipe cleaners, scissors, glue and thin card.

1. Make the front of the glasses from three pipe cleaners, as shown above.

2. Trace the rims onto some card, and cut out.

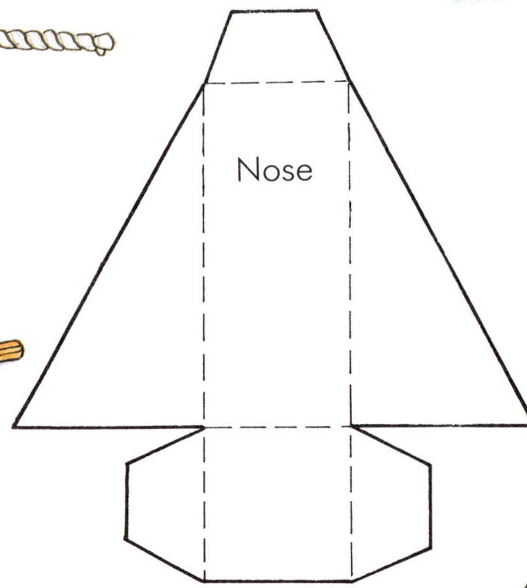

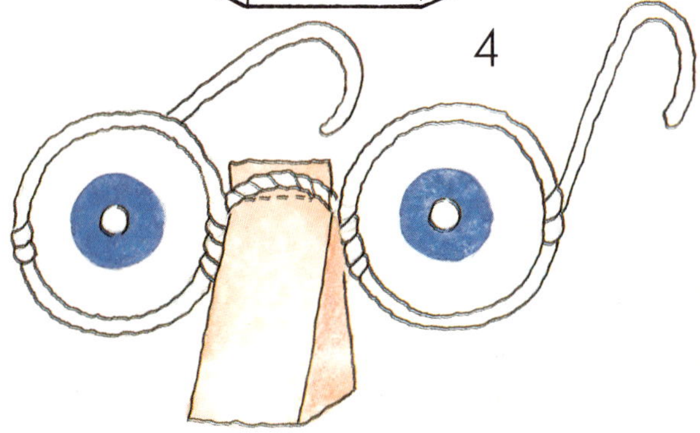

3. Colour the circles to look like eyes and make holes in the middle. Use the last two pipe cleaners to make the arms of the glasses. Bend the ends to fit round your ears. Now glue the eyes on the frames.

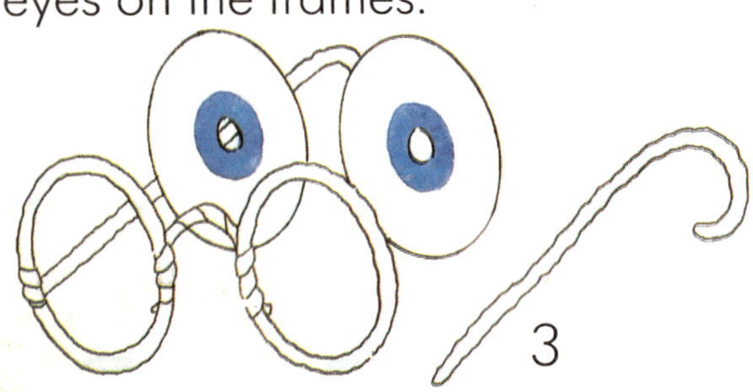

4. Finally, to make the nose, trace the shape shown here on card. Paint it to match your skin, fold it up and glue it on the glasses.

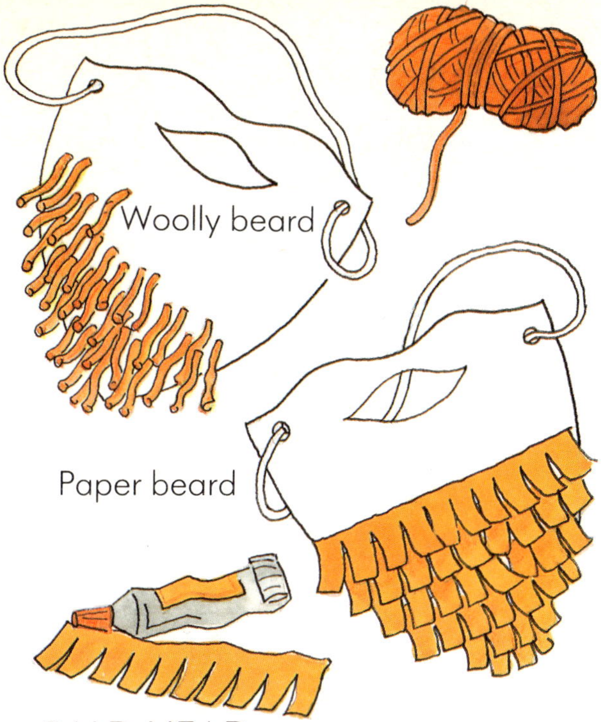

A BEARD

Cut a beard shape out of card to fit your face. Cut a hole for your mouth.

Spread some glue on the card, and stick on bits of wool, or strips of paper cut into fringes. When the glue has dried, make a small hole at each side and thread through some elastic.

A wig

BALD HEAD

Give yourself a bald head by tucking all your hair into a plain swimming cap, as close to your skin colour as possible.

For a wig, cover the cap with glue and bits of wool or paper.

MAKE UP

Ask if you can borrow an adult's make-up for your disguise.

Blot out your eyebrows with foundation cream and powder, and draw in a new shape with an eyebrow pencil. Eyebrow pencils are also good for wrinkles, moles and scars!

E is for eggs

Make breakfast time fun by turning your hard-boiled eggs into funny animals or creatures from outer space! If you want to eat the egg make sure you use non-toxic pens, as some of the colour may stain the egg inside.

For colourful eggs, try boiling white or pale-coloured eggs for 10–15 minutes in water coloured with a few drops of food colouring. Or boil them with onion skins to make the shells turn yellow.

Hard-boiled eggs cut in half can be turned into little mice with almonds for ears and carrots for eyes . . . or make a sailing ship with a cocktail stick and coloured paper . . . or a hedgehog, with chipsticks for spines!

Decorate eggs with initials or names for a party!

F is for flip!

Flip buttons or counters onto the board to score as follows: blue dinosaurs = 1; orange = 2; yellow = 3; purple = 4; red = 5. Score 6 for a pterosaur (flying reptile). Take it in turns to flip – who can score 20 first?

G is for growing

Mustard and cress are very easy to grow, and it's just as easy and twice as much fun to make them grow in a shape. All you need are mustard and cress seeds, scissors, and some absorbent paper towels.

1

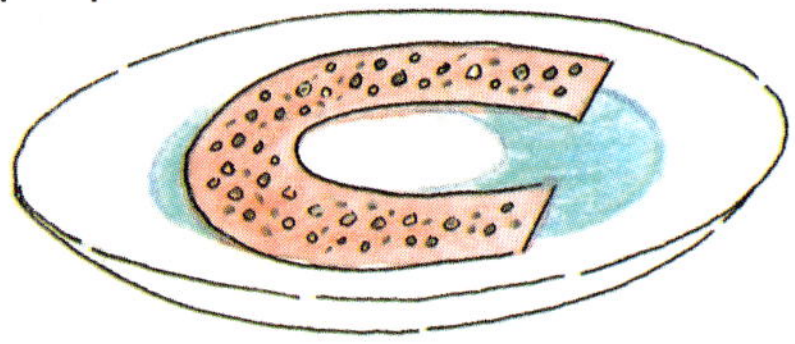

1. Fold the paper double, and cut it into the shape you want. Put the shape onto a saucer, and dampen thoroughly with water. Sprinkle the seeds evenly over the paper, and leave in a light place. You should see results in just a few days. Keep the paper damp.

2. Put damp cotton wool or paper towel at the bottom of an empty carton, or inside half an eggshell. Sprinkle the seeds inside, and draw a face on the outside. When the seeds grow, they will look like green hair!

Try mustard and cress sandwiches!

2

H is for hideaway

Whatever the weather, it's always fun to make a secret hideaway! Spread blankets over chairs, clothes horses or step ladders. Old cardboard boxes with the ends cut out make good doors and windows.

Hideaways are good for those quiet moments when you want to be alone. But you could also think about inviting some special friends in for a party!

I is for invisible ink

The safest way to send secret messages to your friends is by using invisible ink.

1

1. Cut an orange or a lemon in half, and dip a clean nib or the clean end of a used matchstick into the flesh.

2. Use the juice to write a secret message. Write on the back of an ordinary-looking letter or card – it looks less suspicious.

2

To 'cook' the juice and read the message, hold up against a warm radiator.

J is for jellies

Make a crazy jelly! You will need a number of glass tumblers or bowls, and three packets of different-coloured jelly.

Make up one of the jellies, following the instructions on the packet. Divide the liquid up among the tumblers – they should be about a third full.

Very carefully, put the jelly to set at an angle in the fridge. When it has set, make up the next packet and cool before adding to the tumblers. Finally, add the third layer, and leave to set.

K is for knickerbocker glory

Just think of the best ice-cream in the world – then double it! Try some of the ideas given here, or invent your own.

MAKE AN UMBRELLA

To make your knickerbocker even more glorious, crown it with a colourful paper umbrella. Cut out a circle from pretty paper, and follow the pictures.

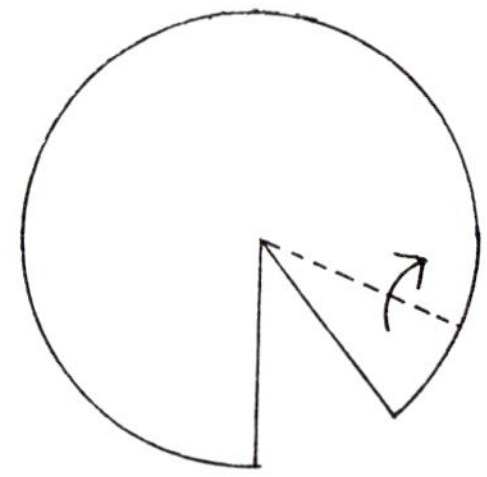

1 Cut out a triangle.

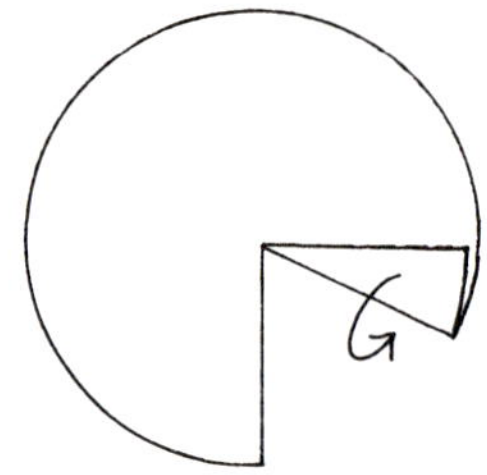

2 Fold it back.

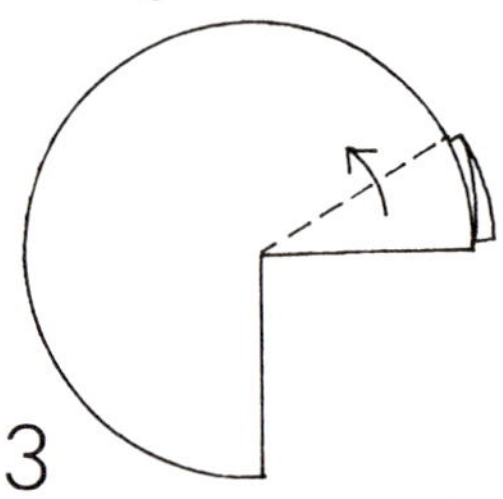

3

Keep folding, to make a concertina . . .

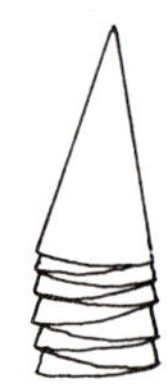

4

. . . like this.

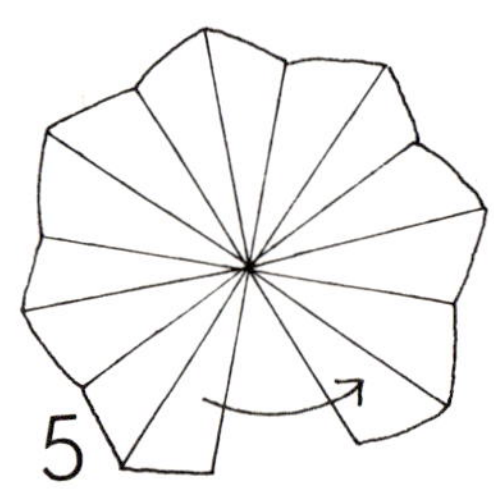

5

Open out, and glue edges together.

6

Push in a cocktail stick.

L is for lemonade

Here's a cool drink to make for a hot day! You will need 4 lemons, 750 millilitres of water, and 150 grams of sugar.

1

2

3

1. Scrub, halve and squeeze the lemons. Put the juice and pulp into a jug with the sugar.

2. Boil the water and pour into the jug, to dissolve the sugar. Add the lemon halves, and leave to cool.

3. Strain the liquid through a sieve. Serve with crushed ice, and top up with fizzy lemonade if you like.

WINTER WARMER

For this winter warmer, you will need 60 grams of fine oatmeal, 1 tablespoon brown sugar, 1 lemon and 250 millilitres of water.

Put the sugar and oatmeal in a bowl. Squeeze the lemon, and add the juice and lemon halves to the bowl. Boil the water, and stir into the mixture. Thin with more water if necessary, and sieve.

This drink is good made with oranges and honey, too!

M is for mouse

Odd socks love being turned into mice! All you need to do is to stuff the sock with bits of screwed-up newspaper, and tie wool around the open end to look like a tail.

Stick buttons on for eyes and nose – or sew them to the sock before you stuff it. Make little ears from felt and sew these on too.

FELT EARS

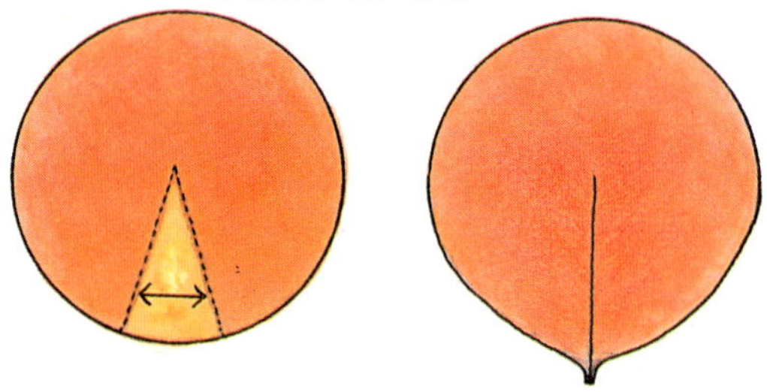

1. Cut a small circle, and put glue on area shown.

2. Pinch together and hold until glue dries.

WHISKERS
Sew lengths of cotton or wool to each side of nose

N is for newspaper

There are no end of things you can make with an old newspaper! Here are just a few ideas.

PAPER HAT

Fold up a sheet of newspaper as shown in the pictures below, and paint brightly for a party – or to make a black witch's hat – or even a pirate's hat with a skull and crossbones!

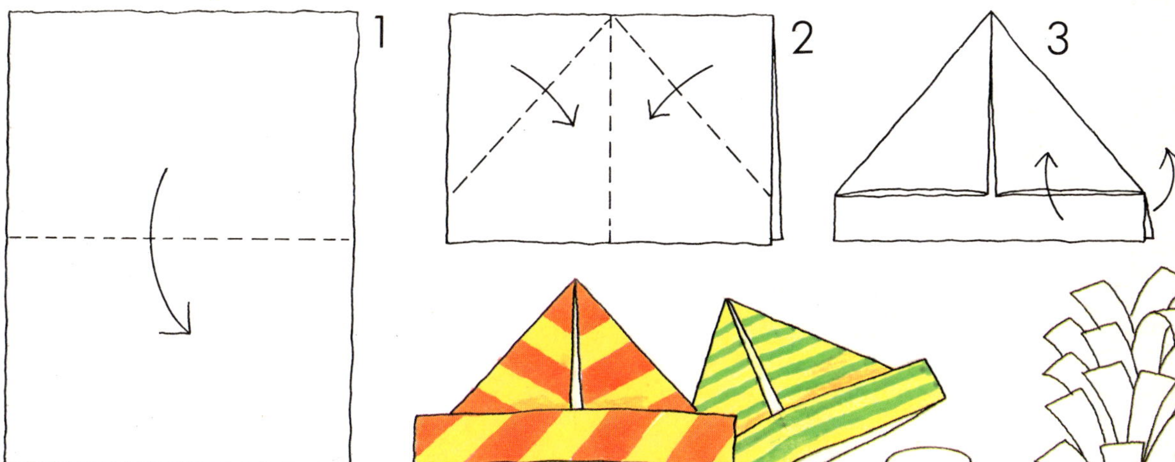

Stripey party hats

MAGIC TREE

1. Roll up a sheet of newspaper fairly tightly. Slip one rubber band around the middle, and one around the bottom.

2. Now make four cuts downwards, cutting as far as the first rubber band.

3. Pull the middle of the roll gently upwards, to make a paper tree.

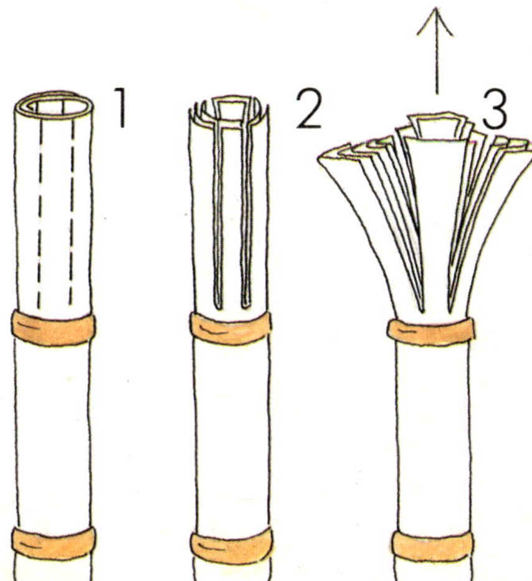
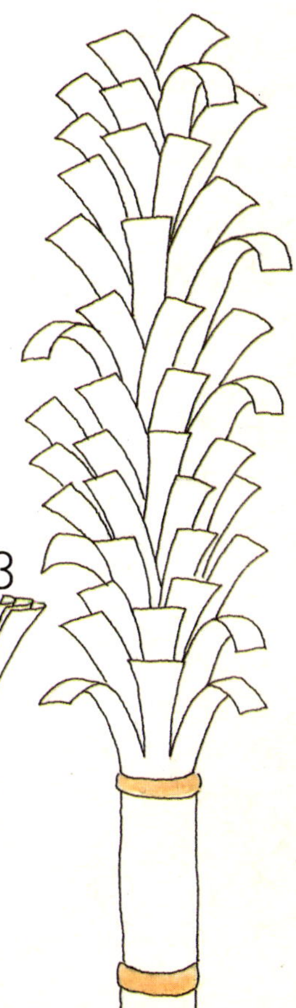

PAPIER MÂCHÉ

1. Put 200 grams of flour in a mixing bowl. Measure out 300 millilitres of water, and add this gradually to the flour to make a paste.

1

2

2. Cover the outside of a bowl with petroleum jelly. Tear up some newspaper into tiny strips, dip them into the paste and stick several layers around the bowl.

3. When all the layers are quite dry, ease the papier mâché off the bowl. Trim off any uneven bits, paint brightly and varnish to give it a hard coat.

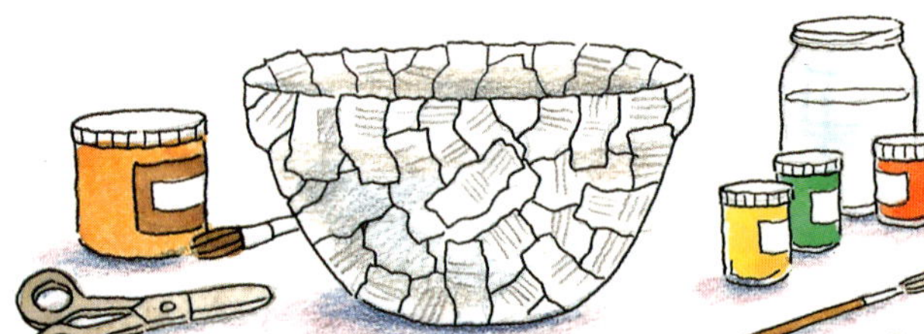

3

Once you've mastered the method, try to think up some papier mâché ideas of your own!

These bowls have cunningly been turned into masks and models.

O is for outside-in

Choose one morning to do everything the wrong way round!

★ Wear your clothes inside out or the wrong way round.
★ Say 'good evening' instead of 'good morning'.
★ Sit back to front at the breakfast table.
★ Put jam on your toast before butter.

★ Drink backwards from your cup.
★ Say your sentences backwards.
★ Say 'no' if you mean 'yes', and 'please' instead of 'thank you'.

Swap places!

P is for postbox

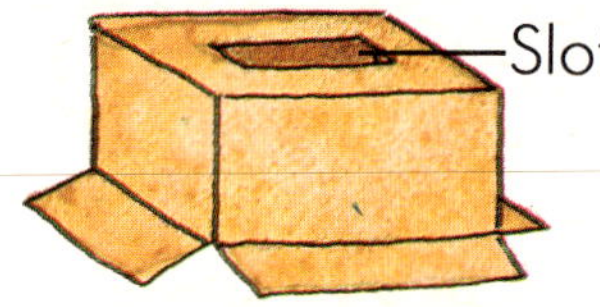

Special family occasions need a special postbox. You will need one big cardboard box and one small one; paints and glue.

1. Fold the flaps of the big box together.

2. Cut a hole, slightly smaller than the opening of the small box.

3. Stick the flaps of the small box onto the big one. Cut a slot in the top, and a flap at the bottom. Paint in a bright colour.

Q is for quick!

Move back all the furniture, scatter lots of cushions, rugs and large cardboard boxes around, take off your shoes – and see who can get around the floor the fastest! You must always jump from obstacle to obstacle, you must go through every box, and under every rug. Can you think up some more obstacles? Check with an adult first!

R is for robot

For a marzipan robot that's good enough to eat, you will need a packet of marzipan, jam, food colouring, glacé cherries and silver cake balls.

1. Cut the marzipan in half. Knead a few drops of food colouring into one half, and leave the other half yellow.

2. Now mould the marzipan into shapes like the ones shown below.

1

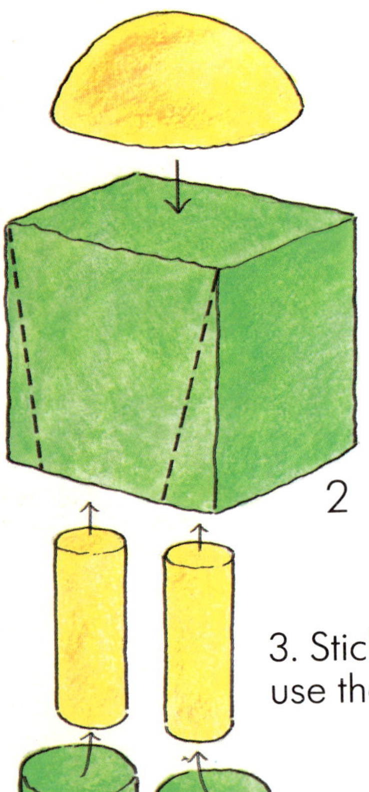

2

3

3. Stick the pieces together with jam, and use the balls and cherries for decoration.

S is for stars

Now you can stargaze without having to get out of bed! Cut out lots of shiny star and space shapes, and ask an adult to help you to fix them to the walls and ceiling.

Find out about the stars and planets. Can you arrange the stars to form some of the well-known constellations (star patterns) you see in the sky at night?

T is for traffic

Who can cross town the quickest? Make the traffic-light spinner shown opposite, and take it in turns to spin. Move the number of spaces shown, and obey the instructions on the board. If you land on a zebra crossing, you must always miss a go.

Use buttons as counters – or make little cars from card.

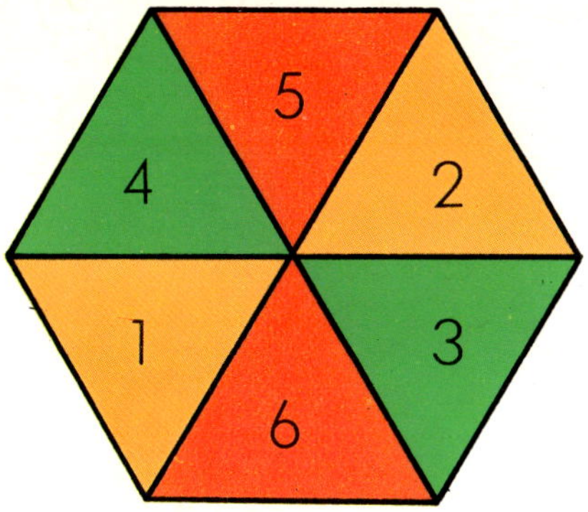

TRAFFIC SPINNER

Trace this shape carefully onto thin card, and paint the triangles in traffic-light colours. Stick a used match through the middle, and spin!

U is for unbirthday

Unbirthdays happen nearly all the time – in fact, on every day except your real birthday! Oddly enough, people hardly ever remember to celebrate these important occasions. Jog their memories by sending out funny party invitations, start making paper chains and party food, blow up a few balloons – and celebrate your unbirthday in style!

Paper chains are made from gummed strips of paper linked together.

V is for village

The models on these pages use matchboxes – but there's no reason why you can't make much bigger buildings using larger boxes. As well as boxes, you will need lots of card, paints and glue.

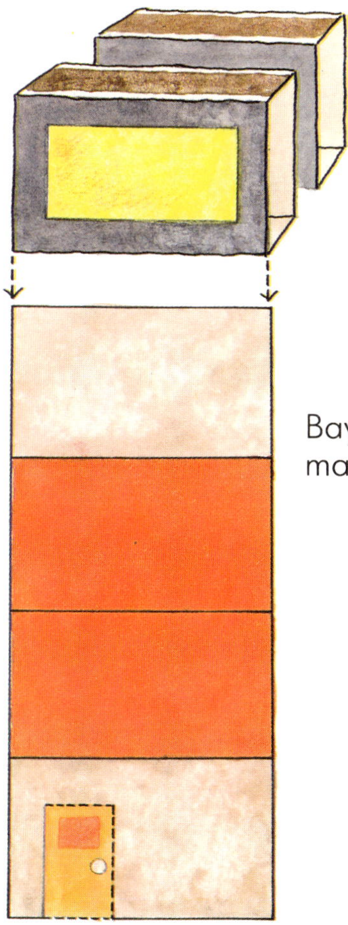

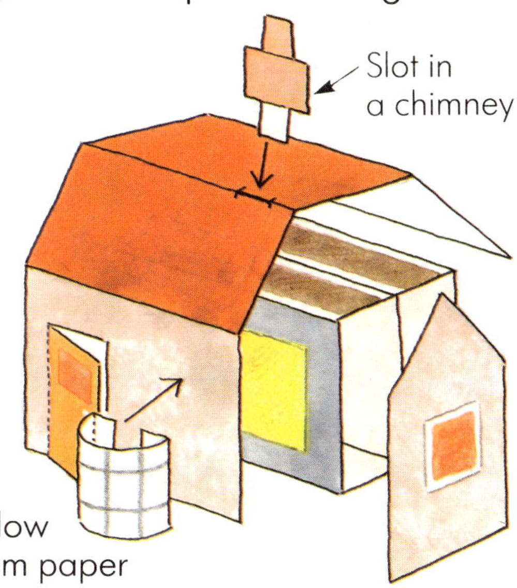

HOUSE
To make a house, stick two big matchboxes together. Use their shape as a guide for cutting out pieces of card to cover the front, sides and roof (or make the roof separately, as shown above).

This house also has a garage, made from a little matchbox

RAILWAY STATION

Give the roof a frilly edge like this. How about painting a station clock on the side? Raise the box on a little card platform, and make a railway line from card too. The flower pots are toothpaste-tube lids, with a bit of sponge painted to look like plants.

SHOPS

Make a whole high street of shops, with everything you would most like to buy painted in the window. How about an old inn with a sign outside?

Hang signs on used matchsticks.

TOWN HOUSE

Turn the matchboxes around the other way to make a house like this.

Put your village on a big sheet of card. Paint in the roads, and make trees and bushes from painted pieces of sponge.

W is for wash time

Bathtime will never be the same again with this funny foam puppet! You will need some thin foam, scissors, a needle and thread and a felt-tipped pen.

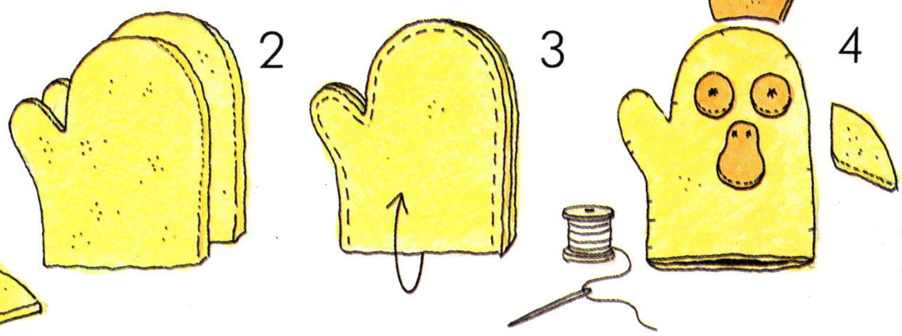

Use the pen to draw around your hand onto the foam. Do this twice, and cut out. Sew the shapes together, leaving the bottom end open. Now turn the glove inside out. Use spare bits of foam for ears, eyes, legs and arms.

X is for xylophone

Take six identical glass tumblers, and fill them up to the levels shown in the picture. Label the tumblers 1 to 6, so you don't get mixed up when you're giving your first concert!

Following the numbers below, see if your audience can recognize 'Twinkle Twinkle Little Star'.

Full | 3/4 full | 2/3 full | 1/2 full | 1/4 full | Empty

① – ① ⑤ – ⑤ ⑥ – ⑥ ⑤ | ④ ④ ③ – ③ ② ② ①
Twin – kle Twin – kle lit – tle star, | How I won – der what you are.

⑤ ⑤ – ④ ④ ③ ③ ② | ⑤ ⑤ ④ – ④ ③ ③ ②
Up , a – bove the world so high | Like a dia – mond in the sky.

① – ① ⑤ – ⑤ ⑥ – ⑥ ⑤ | ④ ④ ③ – ③ ② ② ①
Twin – kle Twin – kle lit – tle star, | How I won – der what you are.

Y is for yawning

Did you know that yawns were catching? Try it for yourself! Have a competition to see who can hold out the longest without joining in. Or try to trick an adult into yawning without letting them know what you are up to. The only danger is that you might find yourself being sent early to bed!

Z is for zig-zag

1

Choose two different pictures from a magazine – they should both be the same size. Now measure a piece of paper that is the same height and twice as long as the pictures.

1. Fold the paper and the pictures into zig-zag pleats – each pleat should be 3 cm wide. Open them out, and divide the pictures into strips by cutting along the folded lines.

2

2. Take one of the pictures, and stick the first strip to the first pleat of the piece of paper. To the second pleat, stick the first strip of the other picture. Keep doing this until all the picture strips are in place.

3. Now fold up your zig-zag picture. If you look at it from one side, you will see one of the pictures. If you look at it from the other side, the other picture will magically appear!

3

Kingfisher Books, Grisewood & Dempsey Ltd,
Elsley House, 24-30 Great Titchfield Street,
London W1P 7AD

First published in 1989 by Kingfisher Books

ISBN 0 86272 425 2

Photoset by Rowland Phototypesetting Ltd
Bury St Edmunds, Suffolk
Printed in Spain